T0125338

BOOKS BY CARMEN GIMÉNEZ SMITH

Milk and Filth (University of Arizona Press, 2013)

Goodbye, Flicker (University of Massachusetts Press, 2012)

The City She Was (Center for Literary Publishing, 2011)

Bring Down the Little Birds (University of Arizona Press, 2010)

Odalisque in Pieces (University of Arizona Press, 2009)

AS EDITOR

Angels of the Americlypse: The New Latin@ Writing, co-edited
with John Chavez (Counterpath Press, 2014)

My Mother She Killed Me, My Father He Ate Me: Forty New Fairy Tales,
edited by Kate Bernheimer with Carmen Giménez Smith
(Penguin, 2010)

CRUEL FUTURES

CITY LIGHTS SPOTLIGHT SERIES NO. 17

CARMEN GIMÉNEZ SMITH

CRUEL

FUTURES

CITY LIGHTS

SAN FRANCISCO

CITY LIGHTS SPOTLIGHT
The City Lights Spotlight Series was founded in 2009,
and is edited by Garrett Caples.

Library of Congress Cataloging-in-Publication Data
Names: Giménez Smith, Carmen, 1971- author.
Title: Cruel futures / Carmen Giménez Smith.
Description: San Francsico : City Lights Books, [2018] | Series: City Lights
Spotlight ; no. 17
Identifiers: LCCN 2017055971 | ISBN 9780872867581 (softcover)
Classification: LCC PS3607.I45215 A6 2018 | DDC 811/.6—dc23
LC record available at https://lccn.loc.gov/2017055971

Cover art: "Untitled" (2018), photograph by Tân Khánh Cao
Cover art © 2018 by Tân Khánh Cao

All City Lights Books are distributed to the trade by
Consortium Book Sales and Distribution: www.cbsd.com

For small press poetry titles by this author and others,
visit Small Press Distribution: www.spdbooks.com

City Lights Books are published at the City Lights Bookstore,
261 Columbus Avenue, San Francisco, CA 94133
www.citylights.com

For my CantoMundo family

Acknowledgments

Poems in this collection have appeared in *The Awl, The Baffler, Best American Poetry 2018, Boston Review, Colorado Review, Columbia: A Journal of Literature and Art, Cream City Review, Feminist Studies, Gulf Coast, Harvard Review, Mandorla, PEN.org, Pleiades, Poems for Political Disaster, poets.org, Poetry Magazine, The Rumpus, The Scofeld, Tinderbox Poetry Journal,* and *Washington Square Review.*

I'm so grateful to Garrett Caples, Chris Carosi, and all the folks at City Lights for bringing this book into the world. I would like to thank the following friends and allies for their support with this book: Rosa Alcalá, Diana Arterian, Jessie Bennett, Mark Bibbins, Wynne Broms, Susan Briante, Stephanie Burt, Adam Fitzgerald, Suzi García, Ross Gay, Dana Gioia, Rigoberto Gonzalez, Richard Greenfield, Sarah Gzemski, Ruth Ellen Kocher, Krystal Languell, Dana Levin, J. Michael Martinez, Farid Matuk, Erika Meitner, Celeste Mendoza, Hoa Nguyen, Deb Paredez, Sandra Simonds, giovanni singleton, Roberto Tejada, Patssi Valdez and Mark Wunderlich. I'm grateful to the gift of time from the Blue Mountain Center and the Hermitage Foundation. And my greatest thanks, always to Evan Lavender-Smith and Jackson and Sofia. I'm eternally grateful to Barry Smith for making so much of my career possible.

There is no one who
will feed the yearning
Face it. You will have
to do, do it yourself.
—Gloria Anzaldua

CONTENTS

I.

LOVE ACTUALLY

When mumblecore
gets eaten by television,
I will understand it better,
then I'll write about it
to create an object that
belongs to no committee,
so it doesn't exist, like
unicorns and democracy.
Then again it won't be
in the art cycle, so you
should write about
my writing about it,
then we'll be the infinity
symbol together projected
against the littered sky.

AS BODY

From a succession of queens,
I was five two and on and on
with the gov. I became t-minus
nihilism, someone's most recent.
I was ten, and then a promise
I discarded for beans. I am fire,
trade fire for maternity,
maternity for majesty—
how sure and freeing to let go
of shackles to trade in for shackles.
I open the door, get opened
by riot. I raise the flag,
got bombarded by episode five.

My body unhinges at the psyche
and suffers a narcissistic
punch-drunkenness,
an exhaustive catalog of sin
inside fits of anxiety and guilt,
occasionally out of range,

braver than the colony pounding
pavement into perpetuity.
A fan of mayhem, I sometimes
celebrate good times by trash
talking the fountain of youth,
straight up jeering it. The night
peters out along with my
resolve to self-improve.

I grew up on the edge
of your electrified fence
like a weed. My brother and I
were a suburban gang and then
trouble magnets, a creed to resist
and abandon, to vex the neighbors,
to disseminate father's grift.
Should have been born pale
scion or with less oddity, less
diagnosis, as I have only twelve
coins worth of goodwill
to spread over my whole life.

I live on the corner of identity
and shadow, one true-false away
from infiltration, grew up
a sinkhole of envy and grunting
want, grew up profligate,
something of a gambler.
Knew when to hold them, when
to wink or stab. Part one:
the gaining on you. Part two:
the ship cast off like the gull's
filthy feather. Oh my god,
this body-boat had been
the perk I promised myself
one day! I was once one and two
and three. I was four and five.
I was all the numbers
until forty-six. I was a first,
an only. I was last.

I want another baby but only
the broad strokes of that anvil
on my head. I'd like the Italian
actor but he is an effort above

my pay grade. I'd love to get at
the so-called insider but he's afraid
of my cha-cha-cha. To barter
is outside my purview. I'd like
to begin loading this heteroglossia
with more brutality, but I keep finding
a new pith: make it even realer.
The self wants to be unburdened
of her bulges. If only I wrote
about robots, and if only
my schooling had been more useful,
but I don't give a shit about robots.
Instead I'm still caught up
with the lyric, that working class
bauble anyone can foment.

DISPATCH FROM MIDLIFE

Gender is the civic center
of my adrenal gland.
I am bound by certainty
to keep it in a shell.
Past fertility, insomnia
is the new membrane
around my nights. My
mortal terror is the now
with what's left of me.
What are you, demand
the witches from the throne
of their own infallible
femininity. I'm a monster
of my own making who quit
one guile for this new one,
wanton with indifference.

MY BROTHER IS A SAVIOR

who   can torpedo
through privilege
with an artistic stun gun
He's a   tempest saturating the city

saws a scar
into the earth   scoops out
an admixture of trauma
and animus   plus
a pinch of   worry from our
adolescent miseries
so he can build   endless
self-perpetuation   literally
with big red bricks

This he does with
our so-called inheritance

We once walked
around our father's force field

looking in   like the matchstick
children

We walked the edges of our houses
to find   a warm window
Was it there
it wasn't

the self-preservation   that hunger
and fear   made me
a bewitching hybrid of
broken coat trees and orbiting
blame and flung doors   king   doctrine
maybe   that elemental
gift of fading into   the wallpaper

The instability   was the brutal
grief of one tornado   while
we   searched for succor
to know its   transport

We're still   looking
plush with hunger

My brother speaks
the cloud's   patois
a hushed medium that loosens
the grip we all wear
on the surface   of his planet
so that we float over the desert
released

More tenderness
might have made us   better
failure   without the sting
less of that grinding down
I said everything   silver-tongued
I left   my brother behind

DEMENTIA AS ABOUT ME

How tidily she hid her illness for years,
which I hereby dutifully record. I write
things like *carved out* or like *guts spooned out
with a rusty spoon*: my guts, her spoon.

BIPOLAR OBJECTIVE CORRELATIVE

Like the spiral
     is symbol for life,
a coil of lightning is how
     I see it, though some days
it becomes a thorn in a lion's
     chest sprouting founts
of dark blood or a vortex
     of self skulking
in recurrent death-dreams.
     Not to die, but to erase
the self from the mind, if it
     weren't for the corporeal
muck. Other days a lark
     breaks through my skin
with chatter and flutter
     and turmoil then—
though my mouth is
     no villain—I get twisted
into a monster. I chatter
     with my lizard brain.

For months some past ghost
        self, then the ghost becomes
an event. 3 doors, 4, then a
        multiplicity—I open them,
until they stack on me
        like blankets in summer,
bittersweet return.

        A cage, a warren.

DECOY GANG WAR VICTIM

Just a tick ago, the actor was a Roman candle
shot to the sky, smudged by rain's helter
skelter. His character was another stooge
on L.A.'s sodden turnpike making art. Got
to rezone and react. The nation: bare wall
to his bullet. Got to rile up the populace, to fortify
the arsenal. Once in a while, repopulate and penetrate,
paint a list of incitement onto the walls.
An elder told him that to overturn the city, one must
surrender body/belongings to the one explosive
spectacle of truth. Pay attention: to overturn
the city, not just the scraps but fervor itself,
not just the wan broadcast of indignation but
IRL incursions into the workhouses and
poorhouses to inflame the thousand points of light.
A lean surge, departure pinks both ends of him.
He's the nth layer folded into the stand's nerve.

DEAR MEDUSA

What was it like to be left with only a stone husband,
stone postman, stone apprentice? Was it loneliness?
A miracle? You had enormous power, which people
called a curse, but it made you one of the first witches.
See, I feel penetrated, and I want to survive my story.
I want to be both vegan and Teflon, Ms. Medusa.
Despite being cursed, weren't your days the wind
lifting swirls of dust around your feet like an omen-cat?
Your deflection cushioned you with a hundred husks.
I want no window into me, not even pores. I write you
because they want to bury my feet deep into the earth
to be loam like that first myth, so your vilification
seems like freedom. I'll end by thanking you for your gift
to pre-feminism. You are truly one of my heroes. In praise
of your impiety and the hiss of your brink, I write
as yr. loyal and devoted disciple. Amen, hallelujah, and so on.

DEMENTIA ELEGY

A million scenes in, I inhabit the sinister
motels haunted with eviction from our homes
on Sioux Street, on Marrow Drive, evicted
from memory too, so split into two levels
of story: one of daymare and the other continuous
present. A burrowing in her head undoes her glacially.
In one moment, we're at our saddest rental
with crooked doors, the balcony peeling with neglect,
and in the next, a shuddering window sends her
into a reverie for her mother's Plaza de Armas.
Dreaming about mothers means mortality is
bristling the hair on your neck. She is all
shipwreck and wind. Her decline is the house
on Field Court where moths got trapped in light
sconces and battered their bodies in hope
until death. I am inside those abandoned
 rooms, swimming in pitch.

VOW RENEWAL

I am afraid for our little nuclear family
since *we* is a delicate and tentacled organism
stretching a thousand light years,
a vortex, a sea and also the bobbing
four-person submarine navigating it.
Once I feared you'd eat through me
with your eyes' wet mouths, so I held
you at arm's length. My worry reinforced
your will, and something like that is
this marriage. Anger in women is not
a negative emotion you said when I was
trying to explode against the flint of your
body. My cock got hard when you said that.
I'd been waiting for you since I was primordial,
so here's to 100 years, my love, and
to our upload onto the same big network.

THE HERO'S JOURNEY

The giant held me in his grip for so long
I began to imagine actually occupying his Trojan
Horsiness. I was always a sucker for shortcuts, and
I only had to persevere through ten crucibles
like when my tail got tipped in goatheads
I used to modify my body into a sieve,
a how-do-you-say for the taking. I had learned
at a young age how mutable the female body
was, everything almost snaps back.

TV, MON AMOUR

Once I was air then screens shot thru
and now I'm an analog surface
Every episode is text text text

I watch therefore I have a seat
at the table of mild conversation
the symptom of thinking
what I feel is significant

I'd like to be honest
about being dissolved by it

Because of television
my material desire
spreads out over the week
I want to buy storage units
tear down walls in my house
birth quintuplets
operate on my face

One day a week I watch TV unadorned
by literary contexts at my friend's
She and I talk about *Laverne and Shirley*
and how we received Laverne
and Shirley as persons

Lucy and Ethel but unleashed
Oscar and Felix but young
and female and working class

My small ambition was to be Laverne
but instead I became like Maude
but not before I was like That Girl

My sister likes to tell me
I'm like Monica from Friends
And like Niles on Frasier
and like all the other tightly wound
narcissist neurotics on television
I think she's trying to
tell me something

Did they just put a Latina maid in
a giant gift box on Suburgatory? Yes
Yes they did

CAREWORN TALE

What is beauty I've been
asking since someone told me
I was/I was not beautiful,
since before body hair and even
before masturbation, which required
no beauty, just the creature
desire for gratification.
I think it was Cleopatra who once
said beauty was the element
of surprise, or perhaps
the rare beauty in my heart
said it because she's chatty,
that one. Beauty is top five
obsession even late in my day.
I pluck stray hairs from my beauty
to assert control over my beauty.
I measure out what I have left.
It is an aftermath, a chariot,
a tax we all pay. I mean
physical beauty, and not of the soul

and I also mean movie ideals
that exempt me for my darkness.
Traces of rage fill my face, then
become my truth borne out as
a category of beauty.
That was a recent revolution.
The moral of the story reads
On the day she truly realized
she was beautiful, she died.

INFLUENCE

Art makes the spider a she,
so we'll go with that.
The spider crouches
in corners, legs drawn
to the spiral of her belly.
She and my mother hiss
at each other, but spider wins
because she's as cunning
as a girl. To my mother, girls
were cherry smears in the rear
windows of a stranger's car,
the situating sinners in
her own mother's allegories.
I played the role of pupil,
the girl in white socks.
Meanwhile the sexuality
of the men that flanked us
terrified us. That was from us,
and also from the world.

FASHION

I finally arrived
at Eileen Fisher
after all those years
of waiting at the door.
What do countries
do to naughty girls? Shave
their beards, hobble
their hooves.

À LA MODE

FOR PATSSI VALDEZ

The still is layers of motif. Upturned and defiant,

all types of shade, no outskirt, vital like a saint.

I once loved two dark princes: one of them spoke

Octavio Paz Spanish and the other sounded like West Texas.

Their gazes were seldom noted in film: anomaly, mask,

some attempt to breach a wall, of being more than nothing.

And the dark angel and her tilt, the erotic halo of her hair.

That uprising. Slick with lipgloss, with legend.

A CASCADE OF FEELING

I was recipient of only thirty percent
of my father's wrath, and that slice
is key to my composition. I'm left
with enough grit to survive, but
not enough to dissolve me.
The prick of trauma is still a pull
into its world, though nowadays
I ignore it. Wrestling with old hurt
or not, I'll still die alone like a poem
reminds me: first night falls,
then the past comes over you.

THE BRIDE

I had a thousand different husbands
once, each a lion tamer, and
unsolvable equation. There was one
with yellow hair who choked me
with his hands and one who bathed me
in a pool and fed me grapes, bought
me silk from Paris. Each husband was
a version of my affliction, but never
like the original. When I opened
my eyes in the mornings of other
husbands, I had to get the light in my
hair right. Settle the sheet over me
like a sexy ghost. I drank glass after
after glass of my own medicine,
practically begging to be newly-formed.

BEING THERE

The wee Yorkie flew against scenery
wet with conjuring. I was dreaming
meta, aware of awareness, the treachery
of thinking. I'm a receptacle
disguised as a person—but still, technically,
a person. The dog was Platonic
in his cuteness, was a figure
in discourse, yet still just a shadow
of the diligent mind I once was,
dense with memes and laments.

RAVERS HAVING BABIES

I tried to make my babies fall in love with
the surrealists but they only want the acid pastels
of the graphic age so the aesthetic pleasuredome
I had planned for them when I was
just an immigrant's daughter corralling future
reinvention from every TV set is dead

Long live my bohemian fantasy of children lolling
over Proust in hammocks they wove themselves
I'll try to let their freak flags fly unencumbered
by my own fantastical wants but pronounce
their slang with the accent of a foreigner
to remind them of their source material

We're at the place where I'm a social hazard
because of everyone suddenly seeing them
thru me I'm still their psychic umbilicus
their status perpetually in flux
Each gesture and turn of phrase
is under scrutiny and I'm hopelessly set
which means I puzzle I perplex I embarrass

Their personalities are starting to be
unchanging like a tattoo and
I remember what that was to feel
doomed in the boundary of self
how little mercy lies ahead

My adolescence floats between us too
and that's the most terrifying specter
that they'll become the worst of me
I was a frantic and edgy teen
who constructed so many urgencies
so many revenge fantasies

like the one about being left the only
girl in the world to set it right
From her own grief my mother cured
me with bowls of rice shiny with butter
or shopping sprees for clothes
we couldn't afford
I wish I knew what her story had been
Now I'm trying to undo it
though I haven't worked it all out
I'm sure there will be pain

Some nights my children wander
into my bed for harbor and I inhale them
in old school want and recall
a more desperate version of myself in love
That woman was all in all hunger
and wanted everything
without question I wonder where she is
now what quadrant her embargo
If only I had known what arriving meant
that saggy tits would be the real story

All this life later through therapy and
also failure I learned that I only ever wanted
the long devotion of family
Oh terrible childhood
what tatters you made of me
though you made me a scrappy little watcher
the breaks are there and vibrate
and make me do stupid things
In seeking love I thought little
of outcome I wish we were layers
we could unfurl as object lesson
maybe that's what a poem is

a flayed skin I can turn into a map
Still crackling I have worked hard
so the one thing my children
will remember is that my love felt
animal and even felt pure as force
sometimes complicated and afraid
but throughout their lives a thread
pulsing with a light they could call my love
Disparate wants and strangers connected
by blood that's me now and I'll take it

What they called false labor was an
exploding supernova of urgency
but it wasn't time not for two weeks
though I felt my child becoming
an insistent storm
like the now-boy in the room
down the hall and then I felt when it
would really happen a pull different
than before an into the relationship
we would have and
there would be an end because life
would always be linked to death

That was the last time I was certain
must be why I'm recalling it
certain of what I needed to do to retain them
That must have been what love ended up being
in the long run in order for me to use it

Every night while they sleep
I'm furled into a ball softened
by sugar and weed trying to solve all
our problems with dread until morning
when they bicker over TV while
time shortens our telomeres without mercy

My kids are just figuring out
their fortunes are pinned to someone
who's a little messy a little loud
someone who isn't going to be a rock but more
of a sloop made of mahogany bobbing in the water
I'll die before identifying a single birdsong
I didn't make them organic or French yet
I think it's too late but we'll live
Ravers having babies was what
Jack said when I told him

I was pregnant and he was only
telling me the truth of my life
the way a friend who has walked
alongside your life
tells you the truth of your life
whether I liked it or not children
would change my life is also what he was
saying we were always marching
in beginning and ending

Like me my babies turn words over
with native wonder
So much to do so little skin
left for transformation
To them the imaginary is still marvel
though each minute inverts them away from me

II.

HOW TO DO IT

I'm fixed to the laptop, bound to the spouse,
in hock to my kids for my career.
'Tis pity, said guilt who acts as diabolic me.
I cook dinner, and she rules from her throne
of razors. Her regard withheld,
she's an ancient predator, so I keep decency
in the bathroom on a shelf with the other potions
meant to soothe my collisions with the living.

MIGRAINE CODE SWITCH

Títere
Títere y título
Títere sans título
The tring tring tring
of Tylenol con la codeine,
tattered tripas and tripping
balls on pain. Títere
in situ, in extremis.
Tres turnos chiflados,
the thrum of cartoons burned
in loops of my tender
once upon era. Opening
a drawer, grating torrents
of fracaso, mama's
in bed otra vez. Vete,
because even breath,
is vampiro. Títere en la torre,
the queen doblada trundled
in the territory, held up
by electric claws in

the reptilian brain as
an oferta to time's scythe.
The angels dig for my teeth
in the sand, then fill
my head with the amniotic sea.

LIBERATE ME

My belly triggers memories of the living and the dead. My belly is a good armrest for texting. I like my belly because all female bodies are intoxicating terrains. My belly: a waterbed for your paternal head. My daughter pushes into my belly button because that's where we are connected. My belly's post-capitalist gurgles. I stroke it at night. *I made this*, I whisper. My belly sets rooms on fire, rhetorically. I like my belly because it is my belly, not quite new a thing. I said *kiss that belly* because that belly will change your life. I inhabit the forest of my belly like an endangered and spotted owl. I hop into a stream, never the same one. I build a fire from the aphorisms from the cherry tree sprouting from my belly button. A belly never stops being beautiful. Alleuia, belly. I love my belly because the insides are all scarred up from living fast. The scars in my belly are workdays and blowing winds and figurative cannibalism. So luxe, my belly. I can think of about five non-related people I would let lick my belly all over. My belly is not political resistance—Alas. This belly of one-woman acts, olive undulations of grain. The fluidity of my belly's size is an assertion of my absolute powers. It's a foxy, round, brown belly. If I could write poems using only my belly, my life would be a different story.

DEFAULT MESSAGE

I have thirty seconds to convince you
that when I'm not home, my verve is still
online or if I'm sleeping when you call,
sheep are grazing on yesterday's melodrama.
Does anybody know what the burning umbrella
really meant? Forget it. Tell me what you need.
Leave me a map. Leave me your net worth
for reference. Better yet, leave me more than you
ever planned. Frankly, I'm anxious your message
will be a series of blurs, that you'll garble
your confession, so I retract every last gesture
for your same retraction. The phone is
in the kitchen, but I've lost my way.

OF PROPERTY

all of my belongings   in the box of my room
enumerated are   books and pages   the stench
of evening body the halo hair on my daughter's sketch of us
glass   of flat diet pepsi   clips of words   prescriptions
photos   checkbook and krazy glue ipad home of my crosswords
lamp and husband hooks briante kloaka and herrera
Bose headphones broadsides tibetan flags
bad to the bone legs   *suttree* hyphenated affliction
Ruthie text   american girl catalog detritus of literary life
the material kind   lines and strategies from husband's books
bled into this din of dr. seuss and smell of a swamp cooler
stacks   called islands laundry in all its states my dysphoria
krystal text today   I peeked into someone else's life
of real wood floors of islands through their avatars
we all   fixate on a palace decent soundsystems
the laptop is my portal   tunnel vision scissors fancy pen
someone else's moleskine I'm lonely   jade plant ikea nightstand
wallet from rosa   notebook from lily   necklace from yael
son's miró-like drawing   the son   my double and my joy
four pillows erratic acquiring and liking strappy sandal in a zappo

44

box: ambien purchase that time somebody scuffed   my face
I objected with a betty boop   mask incense   powerade zero

ALL MONEY IS A MATTER OF BELIEF

Adam Smith

Every poet glistens with the dew
of money, but surely only some of them
truly have it. Never enough, wanting to know
what enough feels like, I buy fake versions
of the things I want on credit, my shelves
laden with zirconia, Prada knockoffs, and
pirated Oscar screeners. I'm driven by envy,
and gluttony, the desire to consume better
than anyone else, but the pleasure is only half
of what it should be, and so on until my house
is filled with objects that belong to Chase
and AmEx. I'd sell my soul, but there aren't any takers.

ANOTHER EXISTENTIAL CRISIS

What has become of the girl writing
her idyll, staring out the window, the one
who fantasized she'd live the wealth-porn
lifestyle of MTV in the 80s? She sits
with *Grey's Anatomy* like a wife watching
Saint Elsewhere. Her eyes are portraits
of nostalgia with the pine trees in the yard,
the red fence. Her thigh gap has become
a reservoir for desire. In the amber light
of watching, the absence of cell phones
makes older movies feel so useless.

TELEVISION PREVENTS ME FROM SEEING THE WORLD AS IT REALLY IS

Simultaneity and Good Exposition are impossible in film and TV!

Workplace shows tout hypercompetence and workaholism!

Soap operas and sitcoms are the genre novels of television!

TV villains have a paradoxical narcotic effect!

Television makes spitefulness in men a siren song, but a venom in women!

Reality television is filled with people who make banality into cash!

My petty Madame Bovarian despair is at the core of all my watching!

Violence is more famous than pornography!

The serial killer is fetishized because America collects everything!

How frangible our women, one choice from death!

Let's bring *that* back on CBS!

VOLDEMORT MANAGEMENT STYLE

Our mute action is full-yes for big mean daddy.

He's going to spank my brown bottom for being a brown baddie.
You can watch
as part of your own betterment.

CNN fawns over the young neo-Nazi with hipster hair.

Dopamine pleasure has a price: liberty.

My price decreased by half this month. I'm a has-been for a
    never-was.

Where's my equal opportunity handout? Where's my Obamaphone, my
    welfare Cadillac?

I ask too late, after the fall.

CONSPIRACY THEORIES

I have seen evidence of a universe
with our same face. This was in visions
sent to me from where contrails
are walkways on the galactic serpent.
I think dogs are a drug, and I also believe
the death of common goodness is a form
of horizontal oppression perpetuated
by the one percent. Phase One: YouTube
comment streams. Phase Two: the death
of innocents for infotainment. I believe
the self-flagellation-industrial complex
squeezes me into a metaphorical training
device for literal training of the body
and the mind, while they numb the part
of my brain where self-love thrives.
I believe in the theory that we build
countless avatars away from ourselves.
My conspiracy theory is hollowed out
of the blankness the screens make of us.
I believe that reunification would

involve some anti-puritanical touching
to start things off. There's one about
an end to buying. I believe that if Goddess
came back, they'd be sent to Guantanamo.
Children are prior to language, the legislators
of the world. Their unformed poems
are prophecies trampled by words.
One more: love is a hologram that disturbs
the air because it is matter. They release
a gas that kills it in us, though the revelation
tell me if they keep it away from us,
it's something we should have,
something we should take.

ETHOS

Now that I know the strategy is grabbing pussies,

I'm going to start a figurative system around

grabbing pussies, and it'll contain some of the spite

I've gathered in the last few years. It'll also include

blood because that's a big part of my work. I'm

going to troll the streets for the insistent root

I need to excise. I have a machete and a hot head,

and you can drive; it's about time. I am close

to setting my girl into the world, more she is

ready to launch into it. I want to clear the dross

of misogyny, so she won't suffer under its yoke.

I'll paint my face, take off my earrings, do the inevitable.

EXCUSES

I write tentative marks in my own blood
and not in the blood of mothers,
which had been for so long
what I had been doing,
a doubling down on doubling down.

I'm all jitters and sadness,
a little messy with conspiracy.
This is a temporary disorder, tho.
I'm heading for recalibration
through the catharsis of art.

Forgive me. The moment
is so sweet, so cold. A new
character, new species of power.
Rough beast in a cheap suit
scales the spire. The thin crust
of money gets thinner and wrapped
in barbed wire. Ivanka, my queen.

OAKLAND FLOAT

I went with Gloria to an isolation chamber place
in Oakland because giovanni had told me that it was
amazing to float, that's what they called sitting in a tank
of water and six pounds of Epsom salt with only yourself
projected against the total darkness, floating. I recall *Altered
States*, the horror of that mutilation, the mutation of who
that guy was and I feel vulnerable to that risk being what I am,
my Mr. Hyde to my Dr. Jekyll. I wanted to know
what I was without the noise of the world buzzing in me;
I operated on two engines, mania and anxiety,
which were a network of screeching dissonance. I had long
told myself to to control it, but sometimes it sparked
out of my mouth or my action verb especially if I was off meds.

In the room I could smell the tinge of bleach permeating
public spaces with warm water: bathrooms, gyms, swimming
pools, kitchens. I worried about the smell in the pod,
but I stepped in and darkness blotted out my thinking of
smell, though I lay back into the salted water to float,
my head on a little cushion they offered as optional

and felt the release in my body of muscles unclenching
and the way my body should feel in the world
if it wasn't shaped by external forces. Unknots, undoing,
uncoiled. I thought it would be like acid, but it was
more like my brain trying to run on its treadmill but
the power is out, so I can't do the things I normally
do in my head, trying to go to the regular sound,
which fizzles out like how a cassette tape would
sometimes play with imperceptible moments
of slowing, then eventually down to silence.

I found five distinct channels and what I mean by that
is in the darkness of the pod there was only sound,
the subtle calming echo sound of water dripping
as in a cave and the sound of voices in my head:
an absolute clamor as I had suspected. One of the channels
in my head was faint: two people from my past a woman
a man and they were the voice of contempt I buried with
this or that, but the ferocity of the hate were the same thready
pitch. That made me feel adolescent or maybe this channel
developed as a result of some hormonal surge in the brain,
this was how we became mortal, living our days with self-loathing.
The next channel was just like an 80s new wave channel

on Pandora, each song barbed with the fantasy life of this girl
I was. The third channel featured an easily distractible narrator
who kept sinking back into reveries; why I maybe will never write
a novel. The fourth channel was pure language, like a floating
alphabet where I was able to turn words into three-dimensional
objects, paragraphs into rooms, books into palaces, so this was
my poetry channel, I guess where I get images and memories
linked to smells, the convergence of all my capturing. The last
channel was an industrial machine built to knead dough
but fractal and it churned at language too, with memory.

I sometimes got bored moving from channel to channel and I was
self-conscious about the occasion of this consciousness,
that it was a part of the bougie industry of relentless
        self-improvement
I had left behind when I fled the Bay Area. Now visiting was fraught
because even specific streetlights on Grand Ave. made me so sad
I could hardly breathe. My brain does that to me, and I could feel
that pain pass over my heart and linger like a bird dipping its beak
in the water of my heart/brain then disappearing, indifferent.
                You play fast and loose, don't you, memory.
I tell my students not to use "brain" or "soul," but I use them
all the time; I thought that too in the float. I was just sparks flying,
but still the sparks were connected and made me extra and awake.

PLACE CHARISMA

I sync my guiding lights
with the memory of dry,
windy heat of cars without
A/C. I take long gulps
of you, California, but
I just can't afford you.

CRUEL FUTURES

Head Bootlicker at Rapacious Inc,
met his colleagues in DC to discuss how loud
us mongrels had become. Dissidents and Uppities,
Jumpies and Haters, all our faces pulsed with rage,
so in new legislations, they'd Botox us with a penalty grin
to show the children what obedience looked like.
We're so not-naughty, so tweet-missiles against injustice, but smiling
on the outside, waiting to pay dearly, subject to change.

USE YOUR WORDS

Alt-Alt-Alt

Borgesian-Waterboard

Candidate Washing

Despotourism

Election-Reality TV

The Funstapo

FurryDeathmatch

Gitmo Towers

Hostile University Takeover

I-Based Economics

Junior League of White Angels

KKK Tax Kut

Left-Wing List

The Men's Rights Candidate

Night Raid Blog

One Last Kiss Law

Perpetual Property

QuikJustice

Rumor Oppression

Suburban Repatriation

ThirdFirst World

Upper Echelon Hazing

Vote Randomizing Hack

Women's Reeducation

XPat app for iPod

Your Little Abortion Texas Funeral

Zero-Sum Subjectivities

FIRST WORLD

A president spills golf balls, teeth and duct tape
onto his desk in his video on YouTube, then
pets his lion. My grandmother once told me how
plutocracy went—not well—and I still meld her South
American political sagas with falling off that cliff called
expulsion in the prayers she led me in every night.
Third World is scary, I had concluded. How was
I to know the snake would consume its own tail?
I could eat and eat and eat them like a volcano with no end,
tweets a puppet, his toupee filled with ghosts,
the Secretary of Whatever sucking his gelid toes.

EGOTISTICAL SUBLIME

I am a boquita,
the sociopathic witch
giving you writer's block.

O my stars.
O my miserable
and cryptic poetry.

Me is a mama.
Me is a descent.
Me is mine eyes.
Me is *so funny*.

Me sane because
I pay a lady for
enhanced cognition.

Tendencies: self-destructive.
Impulses: well-meaning.
My name's etymology: song

and theological promise
corroded by art and sugar.

The first spouse was an oppressor
The second: a divinity.
Each wedding dress
was made of wood:
an admission
of complicity.
The third will be Artemis
because that's my jam.

My stunted yet singular
intellect pushes
against the emperor's
slop. I southern
mise en scène.
Grandmother told me
I'd be a guitar, but
she just wanted
to pluck me.

A SELF-KNOWLEDGE

Being disorganized is
key to my charm.
Being frenzied
is acknowledging
heaven's turmoil:
unruly tentacles into
each nook, each fold
of time and space.
Disorder in exchange
for embracing the now.
Chaotic, therefore
truly logical.

OLD MARRIED

the first kiss   was memento mori   the second one aspiration
the third   audition   the fourth   a posture
the fifth a neurosis   the sixth was   submarine mining
deep grottos of coral   the seventh atavistic   the eighth kiss
a czar from a serialized novel   the ninth kiss was a lagoon
warm as   piano   the tenth kiss   was a month   of travel abroad
we got into   the furred edge of the horizon
the house was empty   for the eleventh   we were alone   and aligned
our   shoulders tattooed   with scratches   the twelfth
a drawn-out   molting   a virtual   hammock
your partisanship   the thirteenth

RARE PRIVILEGE

What my children do not know fills volumes.
It's the least I could do. Sometimes I want
to crack their illusions open because they are
the illusions of the carefree, therefore
the concerns of the children I hated
when I was bucktoothed and hungry for class.
My worst infraction is raising my voice
because that's what being a mother
was. If all goes as planned, when they
undo the ribbon on the Pandora box of
adulthood, they'll only see smiles and low
interest rates. That's what I came here to do.
I still can't wait to hear about their failures,
though. I'll lean in to their face and eat
every word as if they were my last breaths.

LULLABY

What does the poet call
a loss of words?
She calls it widest pupil.
They call it skewed sight.

How precise the nerves
that bear the toll of language.

Once there were stories
I didn't want true about me,
but here I am, twisted

with appetite. My mother
said I was a curious child.
She meant it as a gift.

Pirate moon, the
rapture of deep sleep,
build me a fortress
for my mantle.

NOTES

The epigraph is excerpted the Gloria Anzaldua poem, "Letting Go" in *Borderlands/La Frontera: The New Mestiza*.

"Decoy Gang War Victim" is for ASCO and is based on a photo of the same name by photographer Harry Gamboa Jr., 1974, printed 2010, chromogenic print. The poem "À La Mode" is for Patssi Valdez and is inspired by À La Mode by Asco 1976, printed 2010, chromogenic print. Both of the poems were a part of the ekphrastic project Pintura/Palabra coordinated by Francisco Aragon and Letras Latinas.

The title "All Money is a Matter of Belief" is from Adam Smith's *The Wealth of Nations*.

The poem "Ravers Having Babies" is for Jack Bunting. The poem "TV, Mon Amour" is for Kathyrn Valentine.

"Oakland Float" is for Gloria Maciejewski and giovanni singleton.

CITY LIGHTS SPOTLIGHT